Jennifer Firestone
STORY

Jennifer Firestone
STORY

Ugly Duckling Presse, 2019

ISBN 978-1-946433-33-6
First Edition, First Printing, 2019

Ugly Duckling Presse
The Old American Can Factory
232 Third Street #E-303
Brooklyn, NY 11215
www.uglyducklingpresse.org

Distributed by SPD/Small Press Distribution, Inpress Books (UK),
and Raincoast Books (Canada) via Coach House Books

Design and typesetting by Sarah Lawson, Silvina López Medin, and Kyra Simone
The type is Baskerville with titles in Nouvelle Vague

Books printed offset and bound at McNaughton & Gunn
Cover offset by Prestige Printing

The publication of this book was made possible, in part, by a grant from the National
Endowment for the Arts, by public funds from the New York City Department of
Cultural Affairs in partnership with the City Council, and by the continued support
of the New York State Council on the Arts.

To Jonathan

A beach at midday in a foreign land read as a good beginning.

"White light shoots across the horizon."

The couple assumed their position as newly formed.

"Chairs dig into wet sand."

They assumed an attractive glow acquired from a careful history.

"One page wavering, grainy, damp."

Though the siren screamed we were not there yet.

"She lays a warm hand on the sand."

The books rose up on their abdomens shielding the sun's glare.

"Grainy pages stick, smear."

The water's vastness invited their gaze.

"Colors bleed black-green to cold blue."

The beach provided a restful template.

"His glasses are gold mirrors."

The bar man adjusted his blender, a low noise.

"Sand clings."

Conversation ensued about various plans as a man walked to the other side.

"The ring gleams, oil drops."

A mercurial romance developed as they rightly examined the terms.

"I'd like to take a walk."

Truly heaving the water was, remembering the heaviness.

"The sun ablaze."

The desire to state the weather was perfect was duly reflected.

"Spine sinks in sand, sand flies."

The blaring vehicle suddenly white parked on the sand.

"Ankles hitting warm water."

The lifeguard yelled *rocks* or *waves* or waved excessively.

"Green-blue slabs."

The lifeguard placed dreamily in the sea, a large chair and foam curdling.

"A wave drains."

The lifeguard murmured as milk waves repeatedly washed.

"White under bright light."

The lifeguard watched over or so the story insinuated.

"Gold glasses afloat."

He was the temporary hero set on a watchful throne.

"Running feet, birds."

The water being drunk or splashing.

"Feet weave. Wobble."

The sizzle was sun or was it the camera's quick punch.

"Kelp, a foot touches."

To say they clung fervently to their story isn't quite the truth.

"Adrift, wood sinking."

Like a magnificent sea creature he bounded with his tattered crown upon the shore.

"Wet leaf grips her skin."

There was reason to concede that mythology was futile in circumstances beyond their control.

"He slips through currents."

The white vehicle displaced as it presented later past a pivotal scene.

"His name she screams with two drawn calls."

In thought chambers a comparison: his neck stretched as a quiet turtle.

"Collapses, body smacks shore."

There is a sense that a scream was emitted at the scene.

"Fluttering."

Or rewritten, not a turtle, a wide-eyed fish shucked on land.

"Smack."

That this could be the beginning of a path to which one is destined to adhere.

"Smacks. Flaps."

The transparent evaluation of thought chambers syntactically structuring guilt.

"I'm sorry."

The apology that teetered on renouncing claims to what was once good fortune.

"This wasn't meant to happen."

Incensed to create a heroine dictating through delirium.

"Smacks."

She conjured her grandest gestures as star flowers fell.

"The toe is a petal, an ocean."

To move from space that exhibits discomfort was a natural tendency.

"Sand shoots."

The story frozen as a climactic sequence duly peaked.

"Sand glitters."

Camera clapped a shot of characters otherwise known.

"His wet hand, legs."

Camera's insistent sequencing of stories.

"Tip to right, bright blue."

Time was not tracked, finitely sequestered.

"Tires scraping sand."

The story reverted with nuanced protestations.

"Legs, his wet hand."

If beached adequately, restfulness will be achieved.

"An automobile is an ocean."

Immaculate definition of lounging.

"Rise! Rise! Rise!"

A beach at midday in a foreign land seemed like a good beginning.

"Under the waves, whistle."

The belief that bodies stretched across beach chairs.

"Kelped locks entwine."

Reverting to a filmic space the characters adjusted.

"Unraveled, grainy waves."

She had shot a glance then dropped her jaw.

"Wriggle."

The story shed its encumbered plot.

"Vertebrae collapsed, snapped."

If he were the fallen one who slipped from a sun star then what role would she seek?

"Tongue slackens, lolls."

When the body wriggled like a fish on land, lines of logic dissipated.

"Slim fish, films."

It was like this: she wondered *is this my narrative*?

"Waves crack, pour."

It was like: he said *I love you* and she thought *he's dying*.

"Skin filming."

When the automobile arrived the change of action set.

"Towel snakes her feet."

A denouement any writer would have coveted.

"You You You."

His body was the climactic object disembodied in the sand.

"Spinning dots, flickering."

His body was not his as when he met it close to the beginning.

"Through a glass the sun inhibits."

His body alerted other bodies that trouble appeared and was rapidly approaching.

"Squirm, a sentence."

The story appropriately attentive at this moment.

"Her lips, hand flies."

The story appropriated the beach and paged the rapid sequence.

"My life, is this?"

The story begged the question of whether myth.

"From wedlock, green, shining."

The story thought *should marriage be a principal factor in the impending plot?*

"I'm sorry. I'm…"

The story thought again and said *too sanctimonious* and re-considered tragedy.

"Line up thoughts, label the hours."

The story made his body flip repeatedly.

"What, what is this?"

The automobile motor sustained observing the gesticulating couple.

"White metal."

The driver was written to think *Americans* and gunned furiously.

"Metal breathes."

How would you describe metal mixed with unrelenting sun and salt air?

"Cloud shifts, waters."

Oh is this where you let whiteness do its work?

"   "

You pulled like a postcard skidding across the water but the postcard was an actual wave.

"Wave winces, blinks."

I'm in this and the dive won't pull rare pearls.

"A mouth oh's, opals."

You breathe ice. The throat can hold a chill barely before the page is turned.

"Hiss."

If we're being honest with each other, the story is quite unlike beads of sand.

bead	bead	bead	bead	bead
bead	bead	bead	bead	bead
bead	bead	bead	bead	bead

I will slip away now. . .

"Drops on the glass."

Nighttime etched in quickly as the idea was when darkened all else calms.

"Streams."

Let's sit in this dark place cold but cool.

"Pink shell, tipping."

To stay in this dark cool place was not a sustaining option.

"Spray crab, spray."

Foreign.

"Glass-washed characters, serenely beachy."

Like a screen, cracked.

"Dear, hand me that there."

Permeated she, in her most supple voice (this is back in time).

"Dear, the glass that's near. There."

The waves isolated hovering in their mid-space.

"Water runs, waves."

If he was the weaker, not yet.

"Dear."

Blue weathering in sunlight marched to the horizon.

"A walk, let's take a walk."

To my dear story   gristling in the wind

Line the horizon etching your way as sky

What's in store   a blink whisper   meander   miles

Shuffle and scuttle   erode

The bar man prepared several ornate tropical drinks repeatedly.
Presumably the ambulance crew patiently rattled protocol while lifting.
Presumably another tourist couple hopped into the back with humanitarian kindness.
Presumably the day was pitch perfect and the sea roamed mercifully.
Presumably there was a call to loved ones, a call to a doctor.
Presumably you thought this was your first call in marriage.
Presumably you thought many times *I'll write this*.
A low moan pitched to the deep side shakes itself.

Sand kicks up

A stranger's reflection spoke to him in what appeared to be words.

"Swerve of a footstep curving."

Writing this as one who was once there.

"Silence. Sirens. . ."

The beach if evaluated in present mode was furthest from blank.

"Down the back, a shock of ice."

The story disturbed or aroused the myriad tracings.

"We can start from here, shift to the right."

A doctor in a bungalow approached an inhabited room.

"A silver quarter hovers above a heart."

The words transmuted from phone to phone dissolving in foreign air.

"Flight."

If one deconstructs "honeymoon" one is lifted through multiple zones.

"The sun's blinking its eye dear."

You were a stranger to yourself but strangely more so to your story.

"First, and then second."

She wanted instruction on how to proceed as water cut earth.

"Reflections disembowel."

Who were you with fear is what she thought but was unaware of at the time.

"Action. Motion."

When words are disconnected from action, time is distilled in what might fill one's glass.

"Oil."

When the words are a film scrolling wide over a large body of water the body stills.

"Hush my, my love."

Was the hotel room in the city with the dark wood?
Was the mirror in the city of the beachside hotel?
Was the mirror the mirror he spoke to as in a dream?
Was the blanket etched with the blue running lizards?
Was it the shower or the bathing suit dripping?
Was the chair occupied while he spoke to the mirror?
Was the flowing skirt wrung, hanging on a portable wire?
Was the phone placed on the pedestaled table?
And whom, whom would they call?

A singular stab   inks to the furthest edge

Cover you with blue and blue of blue

Dip plunge   immerse   sting

The sand assembled and reaffixed discretely.

"Slides."

Like a religion where pages fluttered rapidly.

"Her fingers select one still card."

If they stared widely enough a puzzle reassembled.

"Sand and sand so what is the mountain."

The film watched continuously though the hand grasping was unaware.

"A long line raked, obliterates."

When you archive experience it can maintain a time for a certain length.

"Maps her towel. Sands."

The film began and they lifted their nodding heads.

"Eclipse."

Did you want me?

"See."

Did you take me as this?

"See."

He saw a version of himself unburied from a large pool.

"Head contorts, freezes."

His rationality sustained despite the weakening odds.

"Head lifts, forces breath."

We like tragedy in our movies. We like tragedy in our books.

"Wade."

We like conflict, climax, and then control.

"Wade."

When it happened directly it felt obscene.

"A voice unshored, fades."

Or not like us completely but somewhat foreign.

"The fading boat, wails."

They say you see a person clearly in a time of distress.

"Crystal clear, embering."

They say you see their inner being pushed to the outer context.

"Silver with shimmered lines."

Did she behave according to your preconception of her position?

"Locks in place, stills."

Did she emerge wet and coronated, past the sorrows of her human face?

"With grace, murmurs."

And oh tremendous moans as she emerged from the depths of another passing.

"Flits, snakes."

Written as familiar but strangely new.

"Curling."

The structure of knowing how a story is built.

"Stacking."

They shook the film from their skins and tried to break through.

"Lights, atremble."

The film persisted as she watched herself perform.

"Blink. Sun."

Many performances in the past laid the foundation for this future action.

"Wrist. Swivel."

Seeing her acting was how she came to this world.

"Wrist swivels, steadies."

The blinking eye might reveal vapidity or could be extreme fear and expectation.

"Throat. Flies."

Echo a name perhaps echoed across the length of land.

"You."

Desperate calling of a name depicted in many current and former productions.

"But I   was there."

A film is unlike a story, the story desired to be seen.

"A face. Falls."

Her face placid or stretched horizontally as a floating screen.

"White automobile. Unreadable."

He observed his consciousness concerned about her survival.

"One finger, bare."

Certain terms diagnosed such thinking patterns.

"White automobile. Tracks."

The writer likes trauma.

The audience likes trauma.

The anchor that brings her to the steel bottom.

The page is the arms wrapped hungrily toward each body.

The brain withholds this knowledge just enough though a feeling lingers.

The trauma opened up is a salty wound that spreads across her hands.

The trauma opens its mouth, vowels and becomes a drum.

The characters are heavy, logged with water, sand and noise.

The characters would like to drift, swim.

Truly heaving the water

"Slim fish, films."

And like a magnificent sea creature he bounded with his tattered crown

Permeated she, in her most supple voice (this is back in time before

Writing this as one who was

"Ankles hitting

When words are disconnected from action time is distilled

our movies.   our books.

"One page wavering, grainy, damp."

When the automobile

bead
bead
bead

bead
bead
bead

bead
bead
bead

tremendous moans   another passing.

bead
bead
bead

bead
bead
bead

"Vertebrae collapsed,

If they stared widely

"Grainy pages stick

Like a religion where pages

washed characters serenely

Foreign

a version of himself

Or not like us completely but foreign

The film persisted as she watched herself precisely perfo

"You You You."

The sand assembled and reaffixed

currents."

There is a sense that a scream

The story shed its encumbered plot.

"A silver quarter hovers

Swivel."

The driver was written to think

"Water runs, waves."

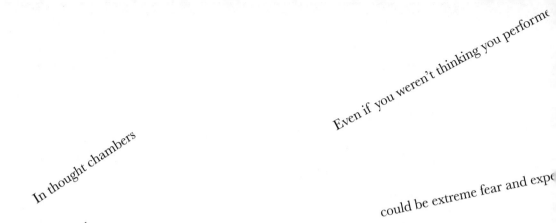

In thought chambers

Even if you weren't thinking you performe

could be extreme fear and expe

wet hand

The blinking eye

"The toe is a petal,

The waves

"Slides."   You   a stranger   but strangely   to your sto

"His name she screams with two drawn calls."

deconstructs honeymoc

ough multip

"White metal."

"Bead, bead.

Bead."

"From wedlock, green, shining."

Acknowledgement that coupling was produced through this chosen form.

"Weighted underground. Lifting."

A breach of contract to be unable to attend to dire circumstances.

"Battling the flies, eyes closing."

A frame can hold only so much figuration.

"Fills. Grainy waves."

The page was at stake when scenery renounced authority.

"The water drawn through."

The camera stole it as soon as you said exotic.

"In an image you are caught."

Even if you weren't thinking you performed it.

"Postcard, curls."

A drill of a whistle inside a wet drum

The story breathes cold under glass

A sentence pertains to poison

The beach splayed open.
The beach crashed upon a mouth.
The beach reached for them but slipped.
The beach shells and sound.
The beach the one syllable until soft.

The story wants to know if you're an artist because you're writing the words.

"Salted crackers, tea."

Are you the writer writing the words so your art is surviving.

"Tea & salty crackers."

If on the boat you ride.
If on the boat you ride.
One wave keeps rewinding.
If a boat arrived.
If a boat arrived.
With wet sand to hands.

And with a curve of a hand the water was mountainous

"Papery."

But that was really her telling of it many years later.

"Paging."

The perspective was skewed so the audience turned toward the scenery.

.

"Specked."

Characters.
The dialogue you quote.
Tension.
Arc.
The shades of subtlety here and there.
They are watching a boat as two immerse.

So the backdrop pulsed paint

Blue   valise cracks

Strewn beach notes

A valise cracking, mouth spitting

The distraction of the frame placates the mind of the writer that writes

Where are you dear story.
Make your entrance known.
Coquettishly refraining from confessing
all parts, the climactic shock.
The cards sprawl and appear
near for telling. When a story
writes itself as one is living it
how complicit are you in its fiction?

A cathartic tug to say what's real
and yet dissolving. Was the sea
raging?

And like clock hands they moved.

"Crowds foaming."

Their memory-dreams advanced at least ten pages.

"Sound of flip."

The huge mountain was just one bird's ledge.

"Gold bracelet, snake."

She understood it was her falseness that nauseated.

"Trickles, the toes."

She understood she wanted it captive.

"Netted, the fish gleaming."

She could feel selfishness originating.

"As a stem, rising."

He had a barren body that wind-swept the land.

"Slashing hips, wish."

He held his camera in his own heart.

"Blackens, clicks."

He would have waved a cape of something but there was nothing.

"Sand and sand."

Their voices were but an ocean drone.

"Like a siren singing."

The white vehicle entering the conversation more than the seizure.

"Gunned."

She had the sense she played the part.

"Rewind. Feet hitting."

What is selected, what is rejected, the remains would like to know.

"Scrawling."

That there were sugar packets ripped and piled.

"Flies and birds, sweetly."

That he spoke to a stranger inside the mirror.

"What, what do you want?"

That there was a doctor in the city who bled his handsomeness.

"Did you ever think it might be post-marital nerves?"

That she detected this doctor felt guilt when he knew she was right.

"He drove around for an hour and couldn't find the place."

That the phone conversation between her and the doctor could have been filmed.

"Bring him in right this minute."

What is the truth but what we say.

"Squeeze, droplets bleed."

The story likes to angle itself as fantasy to tragedy.

"Her hair wet, whirls."

The story is dominating with its ferocious scope.

"His body pulses, clicks."

What she does remember as truth was the feel of an impenetrable screen.

"Run to the bar, a voice thrown."

How could she convey that a newly loved one might be leaving.

"The glance was wild, sea to sea."

She saw a version of herself crouching in the back of the ambulance.

"The scent was faint, like a word."

When you're at the beach you're watching a beautiful film.

"Can you hear the voices, dear."

When you're at the beach you fall in, collapse.

"Dark, except for a square."

When you're at the beach your body burrows and flattens.

"Over there, dear, near the foam."

The beach becomes a painting or postcard, turquoise shifting to aquamarine.

"Zoom to white, blue."

Fragments shift into one placid palate.

"Squares of blue cohere."

He wiped the sand from the camera and aimed.

"Gold, glinting."

The story chuckles as the beach was only the beginning.

"Behind his gold lens, shade."

The story questions was his head cocked to the side as stated.

"Body flips, flipped."

Who was the other couple in the beach ambulance?

"The script, has someone lost the script."

She would not have this. She wanted to get away from the beach.

"Wedges of sand, thick."

She had them leave the beach shifting to the next part.

"Arms reaching sky, clasping."

The beach stole the story or the story stole the beach.

"Words marched a trail."

In front of the screen looming shadow

In front of the ocean salt sprays

In front of blue words fall as they may

It doesn't really matter as this is bound as fact.

"Laces the spine, tightly."

Not fact per se, but a trajectory that is filed as such.

"Frame catches wave catches frame."

He did say he was sorry when he felt it rapidly hit.

"Is that a phone, or hum?"

Solipsistic one's story paging panting.

"Morning time, before beach time, they walk."

What a bastard this story, spreading into the space.

"Before beach, a new couple shines."

The story understands the couple can be moved freely, advanced.

"His hat over one eye, a coin purse."

There was a gray photo album with pictures of them smiling.
There was the photo of the man who sold fish.
There was the photo of her in a big hat.
Of the quaint bungalow.
Of fuchsia flowers.
Of beach people.
Of a shop.
Of a coconut.
Of the tide.
Of an animal.
Of a postcard.

When the body gesticulates as punctuation.

"Half-smile."

When landscape is used as emotion.

"Blue on top of blue=depth."

When language is structured to be excerpted.

"A cloud sinks into a white wave."

Memory believes it is active and operates with control.

"Sand talk."

Memory takes cues from the ego that flails with its needs.

"Turn upside down, watch the sand drizzle."

So many stories that any given day can be told.

"Bodies sit down and language delivers."

ACKNOWLEDGMENTS

Acknowledgement and thanks to editors who published selections from *STORY* in earlier versions: E•ratio, *Prelude*, *TAG*, and *TYPO*.

Deep thanks to everyone at Ugly Duckling Presse, especially my insightful, attentive editors, Silvina López Medin and Kyra Simone, and the wonderful designer, Sarah Lawson.

Special thanks to Kate Greenstreet for her thoughtful feedback, and Max and Kate Greenstreet for creating the short film that corresponds to *STORY*.

Thanks also to the early readers of this work: Brenda Coultas, Marcella Durand, Amanda Field, Erica Hunt, Katy Lederer, Caitlin McDonnell, Carley Moore, Idra Novey, Lynn Melnick, Laura Sims, Leah Souffrant, and to Carla Harryman, Eugene Lim, Laura Y. Liu, Dana Teen Lomax, Rachel Levitsky, Jill Magi, Albert Mobilio, Sarah Rosenthal, Henry Shapiro, Ann Snitow, Joanna Sondheim, Karen Weiser, and Leni Zumas for their love and support, and to my loving family, Jonathan, Ava, Judah, and Iris.